Piece = Part = Portion
Pedazo = Parte = Porción

Fractions = Decimals = Percents
Fracciones = Decimales = Porcentajes

BY/POR **Scott Gifford**

PHOTOGRAPHS BY/FOTOGRAFÍAS DE **Shmuel Thaler**

TRICYCLE PRESS
Berkeley | Toronto

Hello Hola Bonjour

Each of these words mean the same thing—a friendly greeting—in a different language.

Estas tres palabras significan lo mismo, un saludo amistoso, en distintos idiomas.

Glad   Merry   Joyful

Each of these words refers to the same thing—a happy feeling—in a slightly different way.

Contento   Alegre   Feliz

Estas tres palabras describen algo parecido, un sentimiento de felicidad, de una manera un poco diferente.

Fractions   Decimals   Percents

Each of these words describes the same thing—a part of something—by a different name.

Fracciones   Decimales   Porcentajes

Estas tres palabras describen lo mismo, una parte de algo, con un nombre diferente.

Fractions look like this: $\frac{1}{2}$
and sound like this: one half

Las fracciones son así: $\frac{1}{2}$
y se leen así: un medio

Decimals look like this: .50
and sound like this: fifty hundredths

Los decimales son así: .50
y se leen así: cincuenta centésimos

Percents look like this: 50%
and sound like this: fifty percent

Los porcentajes son así: 50%
y se leen así: cincuenta por ciento

The fraction $\frac{1}{2}$ means "1 divided by 2". To find the decimal version of $\frac{1}{2}$, divide 1 by 2 and the result is the decimal .50.

La fracción $\frac{1}{2}$ significa "1 dividido por 2". Para saber el decimal de $\frac{1}{2}$, se divide 1 por 2 y el resultado es el decimal .50.

$$\frac{1}{2} = 2\overline{)1.00}^{.50}$$

$$\frac{1}{2} = 2\overline{)1.00}^{.50}$$

To find the percent version of .50, multiply .50 by 100 ("percent" means "for each hundred"), add a percent sign and the result is 50%.

Para encontrar el porcentaje de .50, multiplica .50 por 100 ("porcentaje" significa "por cada cien"), añade el signo del porcentaje y el resultado es 50%.

$$.50 \times 100 = 50\%$$

$$.50 \times 100 = 50\%$$

It often seems as though fractions, decimals, and percents are three separate, unconnected ideas. But fractions are used for more than just to show parts of things. Decimals are not only used when working with money. And percents can be used for much more than just calculating sales tax and interest.

Muchas veces parece que las fracciones, los decimales, y los porcentajes son tres conceptos separados que no tienen relación entre sí. Pero las fracciones se utilizan para más cosas que para mostrar las partes de un todo. Los decimales no sólo se usan al hablar de dinero. Y los porcentajes se pueden usar para muchas más cosas que para calcular el impuesto a la venta y los intereses.

In the language of mathematics, fractions, decimals, and percents are three different, but connected, ways of describing the same parts of things.

En el lenguaje de las matemáticas, las fracciones, los decimales y los porcentajes son tres maneras distintas, pero relacionadas, de describir las mismas partes de algo.

$\dfrac{1}{2}$ of a pair of shoes

de un par de zapatos

.50

50%

$$\frac{1}{12}$$

of a dozen eggs
de una docena de huevos

.08   8%

$$\frac{1}{11}$$

of a soccer team

de un equipo de fútbol

.09   9%

$$\frac{1}{10}$$

of your toes

de los dedos de tus pies

.10   10%

$$\frac{1}{9}$$

of a tic-tac-toe game
del juego tres en raya

.11   11%

$$\frac{1}{8}$$

of a pie

de un pastel

.125   12.5%

$$\frac{1}{7}$$

of a week

de una semana

.14   14%

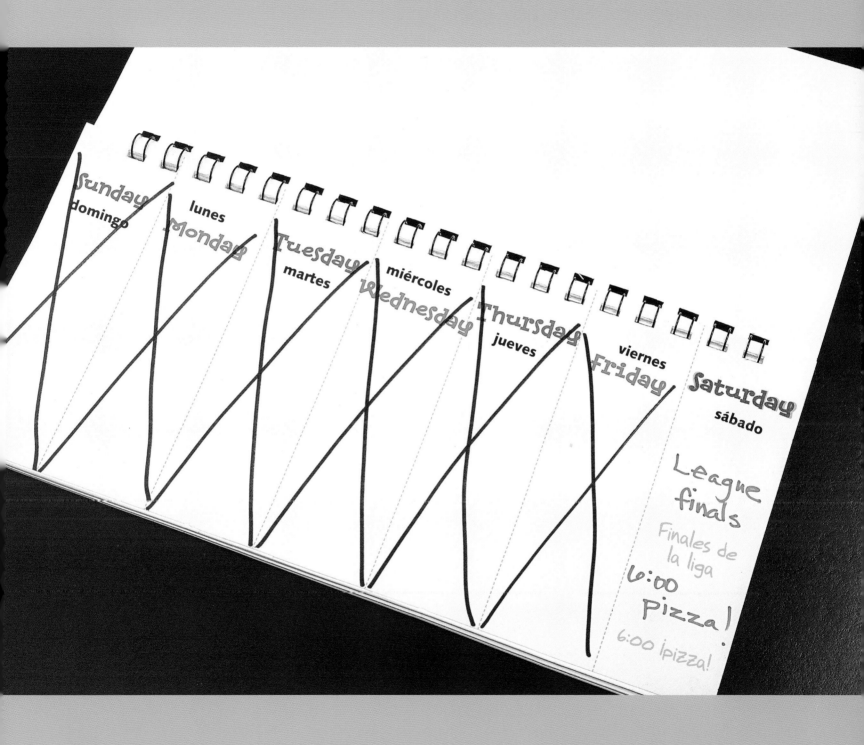

$$\frac{1}{6}$$

of a six-pack

de un paquete de seis refrescos

.166   16.6%

$$\frac{1}{5}$$

of a pack of gum

de un paquete de chicle

.20   20%

$$\frac{1}{4}$$

of a dollar

de un dólar

.25   25%

1796 - Tennessee - 2002

1803 - Ohio - 2002

1818 - Illinois - 2003

1819 - Alabama - 2003

$$\frac{1}{3}$$

of a traffic light
de un semáforo

.33   33 %

$$\frac{2}{3}$$

of a place setting

de un servicio de cubiertos

.66   66%

$$\frac{3}{4}$$

of a sandwich
de un sándwich

.75   75%

$$\frac{99}{100}$$

of a dollar
de un dólar

.99   99%

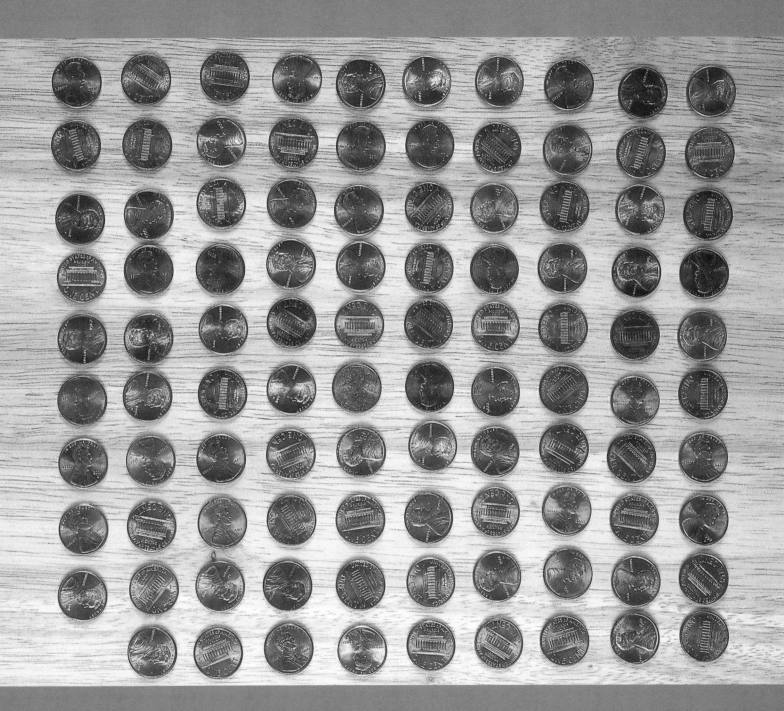

1

whole pizza

una pizza entera

1.00   100%

This is for my students at Fremont Open Plan, who inspired the idea.—SG

To my wife Kathy and daughters Kayla and Hannah—the fractions in my life that are far greater than the sum of the parts.—ST

Este libro es para mis estudiantes de Fremont Open Play, que me inspiraron con esta idea.—SG

A mi esposa Kathy y a mis hijas: Kayla y Hannah, las fracciones de mi vida que son mucho más grandes que la suma de sus partes.—ST

· ·

Text copyright © 2003 by Scott Gifford
Photographs copyright © 2003 by Shmuel Thaler
Spanish translation copyright © 2007 by Tricycle Press
Spanish translation by Aurora Hernandez

Tricycle Press
an imprint of Ten Speed Press
PO Box 7123
Berkeley, California 94707
www.tricyclepress.com

Design by Catherine Jacobes
and Katy Brown
Typeset in Syntax

First English language printing, 2003
First bilingual printing, 2007
Printed in Singapore

1 2 3 4 5 6 — 12 11 10 09 08 07 hc
1 2 3 4 5 6 — 12 11 10 09 08 07 ppk

Library of Congress Cataloging-in-Publication Data
Gifford, Scott, 1955-
    Piece=part=portion : fractions=decimals=percents / by Scott Gifford ; photographs by Shmuel Thaler.
        p. cm.
Summary: Explains how in the language of mathematics, fractions,decimals and percents are three different ways of describing the same parts of things.
    ISBN 978-1-58246-225-7 bilingual hc
    ISBN 978-1-58246-226-4 bilingual ppk
1. Fractions—Juvenile literature. 2. Logic, Symbolic and mathematical—Juvenile literature. [1. Fractions. 2. Decimal fractions. 3. Percentage.] I. Thaler, Shmuel, ill. II. Title.
    QA117.G54 2003
    513.2'6—dc21
                            2003006118